Y0-DOK-385

HELPING CHILDREN UNDERSTAND THEIR FEELINGS

A Practical Resource Guide for *Sometimes I Feel Awful*

By Joan Singleton Prestine

Fearon Teacher Aids
A Division of Frank Schaffer Publications, Inc.

Editorial Director: Virginia L. Murphy

Editor: Carolea Williams

Copyeditor: Lisa Schwimmer

Cover and Inside Illustration: Virginia Kylberg

Design: Marek/Janci Design

Cover Design: Lucyna Green

This Fearon Teacher Aids product was formerly manufactured and distributed by American Teaching Aids, Inc., a subsidiary of Silver Burdett Ginn, and is now manufactured and distributed by Frank Schaffer Publications, Inc. FEARON, FEARON TEACHER AIDS, and the FEARON balloon logo are marks used under license from Simon & Schuster, Inc.

© **Fearon Teacher Aids**
A Division of Frank Schaffer Publication, Inc.
23740 Hawthorne Boulevard
Torrance, CA 90505-5927

Entire contents copyright © 1993 by Fearon Teacher Aids, 23740 Hawthorne Blvd. Torrance, CA 90505. However, the individual purchaser may reproduce designated materials in this book for classroom and individual use, but the purchase of this book does not entitle reproduction of any part for an entire school, district, or system. Such use is strictly prohibited.

Library of Congress Catalog Card Number: 93–72029

ISBN 0-86653-926-3
Printed in the United States of America
1. 9 8 7 6

Acknowledgments

I want to thank the following people for their support, encouragement, and expertise. Their suggestions were invaluable.

Doug Prestine, my husband, best friend, and computer expert

Ginger Murphy, editorial director and ego booster

Carolea Williams, editor and advisor

Lisa Schwimmer, copyeditor and good listener

Virginia Kylberg, gifted artist

Marek/Janci Design and Lucyna Green, whose cover and book designs brought the words to life

Patsy Loyd, Sales Manager for Fearon Teacher Aids

Sandy Hatch and Ann Alper, marriage, family, and child counselors

Debbie Kachidurian, Joann Burch, and Davida Kristy, teachers

Jeffrey Prestine, Communications Major

Nadine Davidson, Celeste Mannis, and Karen Eustis, fellow authors

Frances Singleton and Joanne Singleton, wise beyond their years

Herb Singleton, Scott and Laurie Prestine, John Singleton, Geraldine Prestine, and Jim Kachidurian, loyal supporters

Contents

Preface

So often children bury or cover their feelings because they are too frightened to describe or share them. Children may fear that others won't like them because of their feelings or may be critical towards them if their feelings are unusual or different. Adults don't always know how to react to children's feelings. Often, adults are still trying to "fix" their own feelings. Consequently, they don't know how to deal openly with children's feelings when these feelings are threatening to their own sense of security. Ironically, most children just want someone to listen quietly to them.

Helping Children Understand Their Feelings was written to help young children openly communicate their inner feelings. This book was also intended to help adults become better listeners and share with children the notion that all feelings are okay—even feelings considered "bad" by others. It is my hope that children can feel comfortable sharing their feelings with those with whom they live, play, study, and interact. It is my hope, too, that adults can use the ideas presented here to offer healthy alternatives to "stuffing" or ignoring children's feelings or behaviors.

About *Sometimes I Feel Awful*

The *Sometimes I feel Awful* picturebook is designed to help children identify and deal with various emotions. Read the book and discuss the story with children as a prelude to using the activities outlined in this resource.

In the story, a little girl begins her day feeling happy. Through a series of actions, she experiences a variety of feelings and emotions and responds to these emotions in many ways. She feels jealous when her mother gives more attention to her sister. She feels impatient with her friend, David. She feels frightened when she climbs a tree and the branches start to sway. She feels shy when her brother brings a new friend home. And, she feels left out when her mom and her brother seem to be ignoring her. The story points out that communication is the key to dealing with emotions. At the end of the story, the little girl realizes that she needs to tell those around her how she is feeling if she expects people to understand her.

Introduction

Emotions are natural to every growing child. Feelings and emotions are just as strong in children as they are in adults. As adults, we need to remember to listen to the feelings and thoughts of children. We may not understand the intensity of children's feelings, but a child's emotions are very real to him or her. If we view children as the feeling, thoughtful individuals that they are, we can enrich our own lives as well as theirs.

It is unhealthy to try to stem or control children's emotions. Sometimes all a child needs is a little space or quiet time to take a deep breath and relax when things don't seem to be going well. Or, sometimes children just need affection or reassurance that they are cared for. Adults can learn how to help children deal with their emotions in helpful and positive ways. They need to understand that it is okay to feel mad, sad, frustrated, shy, or cranky. We can also teach children that they have the ability to choose to respond negatively or positively to their feelings.

Listening to something is very different from simply hearing. A level of trust develops as children realize that you listen and care about what they have to say. When listening to a child, try to position yourself at eye level. Sit on a small chair or kneel beside the child. Standing conveys a sense of urgency, as though you don't have the time to listen. You are on more equal terms at a child's eye level. After careful listening, it is then possible for you to help a child clarify his or her feelings.

Be careful not to tell children how they should feel or respond. Like adults, children's feelings are their own. You can help by listening and encouraging them to share their feelings with you.

This resource guide is intended to help children understand their emotions and realize that it is normal to have many different feelings and many different responses. It is equally important that adults are able to communicate and listen to children. We can teach children that every action leads to a certain feeling or emotion. And when children feel a certain way, they respond in some way to that feeling. Actions evoke feelings and those feelings bring about responses. This cycle—action, feeling, response—is universal.

Helping Children Understand Their Feelings is a guide to help teachers, parents, and other adults assist children in understanding and dealing with the many emotions they will experience. This resource provides practical suggestions and activities for communicating with children, recognizing their emotions, and helping children learn to respond in constructive, positive ways to the fourteen emotions presented in the picturebook *Sometimes I Feel Awful*.

Relationships

The relationships in children's lives play a large part in how children learn to respond to their own feelings. Each relationship is important—parent/child, teacher/child, as well as relationships with siblings and friends. All help to mold children's attitudes towards their feelings.

Parent/Child

Because children are dependent, parents have tremendous power over how children respond to their own feelings. By the time they are toddlers, children have learned how they are to respond to actions by modeling the behaviors of their parents. Sometimes the learned behavior is negative.

Parents who show indifference toward their children tend to have children with lower self-esteem, while parents who interact often with their children usually have children who feel better about themselves. Children's self-esteem seems to be affected more positively by parental interaction than by socio-economic standing, physical appearance, or intelligence. A parent's positive interaction with a child is essential to good self-esteem. If children feel love, respect, and acceptance from their parents, they usually feel the same for themselves and are more able to love, respect, and accept others.

Brothers and Sisters

Children not only model the behavior of their parents, but of their siblings as well. Every family is different. In some families, siblings are best friends. In other families, children spend much of their childhood pinching, poking, punching, belittling, name calling, and tattling. This can be trying on parents, teachers, and others, but especially on the children.

Sibling rivalry may lower self-esteem, attitude, and motivation if siblings choose to respond negatively toward one another. Children can't choose their families, but they can choose to respond by making the best of their families and accepting each other's strengths and weaknesses.

Friends

Even though children may be good friends, sometimes it's difficult for them to share their feelings. Friends are important to children and some children feel that disclosing their feelings to their friends may jeopardize their friendship. Some feel their friends may not understand. Others are afraid of being teased. It doesn't occur to some children to share their feelings, while others want to keep their feelings to themselves.

In order for most children to have high self-esteem and comfortable feelings, they need acceptance from their peers—but children can be tough critics. They judge each other on many levels—athletic ability, intelligence, personality, looks, and size, to name just a few. Children don't always respond kindly towards one another. When one child is unhappy with another, they may sometimes hurt each other's feelings by responding critically or bringing up something they may have learned in confidence.

Teacher/Child

It is difficult for some children to understand why a teacher can't always respond to their immediate needs. Some children may feel they are not receiving the attention they need and respond by becoming loud and aggressive. Others may whine and nag, while others may become quietly withdrawn.

Regardless of how they respond, some children enter a classroom with a previous history. They fall into behaviors they have learned at home or in other classrooms, such as class clown, talkative, aggressive, athletic, quiet, loud, mature, immature, smart, stupid, slow, fast, and so on. Some children try to improve their image by changing their responses. Occasionally teachers are unaware of the attempted changes, so the children continue to feel uncomfortable and fall back into their old behaviors.

It's important to remind children that no one knows how they feel unless they share their feelings—adults can't see into their heads or guess how children might be feeling.

The Emotion Cycle

It's important for children to understand that feelings don't just happen. There is a reason that children feel the way they do and feelings can be a response to an action, event, situation, activity, or person. Feelings aren't random. Children need to know that whatever they are feeling is an honest result of what is going on around them. These emotions are not wrong—it's okay for children to feel their feelings.

What we need to do, as adults, is teach children how to respond to their feelings in healthy ways. By teaching children that their responses have natural consequences, children begin to learn to choose appropriate responses. Children often do not understand logical thinking until they are 6 or 7 years old. Thus, preschool and kindergarten children do not always clearly understand that they have choices in their responses.

Actions

Actions begin the emotion cycle. There are three main types of actions. The first is a physical action, such as receiving a hug or falling off a chair. For example, if Mom gives Tina a hug, Tina feels loved. The second type of action is visual. If Lisa sees José take her ball, she feels angry. The third type of action is auditory—hearing someone within one's environment. If Pedro hears Michael say he is smart, Pedro feels proud. Help children understand the concept that actions make them feel an emotion, and in turn, they respond to that emotion.

Action List

List the following feelings on the chalkboard or on chart paper—happy, jealous, impatient, selfish, angry, frightened, sad, cranky, lonely, frustrated, ashamed, shy, left out, and tired. Invite children to think of things that have happened that caused them to feel each emotion. Record the children's ideas on the chalkboard. Or, invite younger children to draw pictures of the actions. Encourage children to identify each action as something they feel, see, or hear.

Positive Actions

Make an effort to notice the positive actions of children and encourage them to notice their own good qualities as well. Children need constant reminders of how special they are. Give each child a shoebox with a lid. Suggest that children paint the boxes with bright colors and write their names on the bottoms. Give each child several slips of brightly colored paper. Invite children to write or draw pictures of their own actions that they feel good about. Add ideas of your own to each child's box. Pick a special time to sit with each child and read through his or her box full of accomplishments.

Feelings

So many times, adults, especially parents, want to make their children feel better, take away hurtful feelings, or shelter children from uncomfortable feelings. It's not within anyone's power to make uncomfortable feelings go away for children. Adults can guide and help children understand their feelings, but ultimately it's up to the children to work through their feelings and choose how they will respond to those feelings. We can help children learn that they can control their feelings, rather than letting their feelings control them. Stress that controlling feelings does not mean suppressing feelings—controlling feelings means recognizing, accepting, and expressing one's feelings in positive ways.

Some children learn to turn off their feelings—others learn that certain feelings are all right to express and others are not. Some children are open and willing to share most of their feelings. Children need to know that it's okay to express the way they feel—no one can crawl into their heads to know how they are feeling and no one knows what they are thinking. We can see angry actions, but not angry feelings. In order for others to know how they feel, children need to express themselves clearly.

The best gift you can give children is an understanding of their feelings, the ability to tell others how they feel, and the freedom that allows them to share their feelings with others.

Explain to children that there are many types of feelings. There are comfortable feelings, such as joy, love, or pride, and there are uncomfortable feelings, such as sadness, frustration, or anger.

Comfortable Feelings

Describe a comfortable situation to children, such as riding a bike or putting a puzzle together. Invite children to list feelings that make them feel comfortable. Children may include the words happy, peaceful, proud, silly, relieved, and content in their lists. Invite younger children to draw pictures of their feelings.

Uncomfortable Feelings

Describe an uncomfortable situation to children, such as not being able to hit a ball or having problems coloring a picture. Invite children to list or draw feelings that make them feel uncomfortable. Children may include feelings, such as angry, frustrated, lonely, and embarrassed, in their lists or drawings.

My Feelings and Me

Ask children the following questions and invite them to write or draw a response.
- Who decides how you feel?
- Who is in charge of your feelings?
- Who do your feelings affect?
- Who do you tell your feelings to?

Help children see that they are ultimately responsible for their own feelings and that they can make good choices about how to respond to their feelings.

Sharing Feelings

Have children make a list or draw pictures of the feelings they felt yesterday. Invite children to draw happy faces next to the feelings they shared with someone else. Suggest that children put sad faces next to the feelings they did not share. Encourage children to consider whom they feel most comfortable sharing their feelings with and to make an effort to talk about their feelings with others.

Feeling Faces

It is difficult for many children to put feelings into words or to express their feelings constructively. Give each child several paper plates. Invite children to draw pictures on their plates that represent emotions. Help each child write the name of the emotion underneath each drawing. Make a hole in the top of each child's assortment of paper-plate faces. String each child's plates onto a piece of yarn. Encourage children to flip their plate faces to show how they are feeling. Each child can also share his or her feelings with others at home by hanging the appropriate feeling face on a door knob, refrigerator, or desk. Invite children to share their feelings verbally as well.

Responses

Everyone experiences actions and everyone has feelings about those actions. The difference is that everyone responds differently to the different actions and feelings. Life is a series of challenges. The way children choose to respond to these challenges is the way they choose to live their lives. Children who generally respond negatively often feel like failures. If children choose to think of negative actions and feelings as challenges, not problems, they tend to respond more constructively and move forward. Children who generally respond positively enjoy new challenges and tolerate temporary setbacks. They usually take pride in their responses. Help children understand the connection between feelings and responses with the following activities.

Feeling and Responding Game

Some children get so caught up in actions or feelings that it is difficult for them to respond appropriately. Invite children to use the feeling faces (see page 16) they made to play a game that gives them practice responding to actions in constructive ways. Encourage each child to display one of the feeling faces and draw a picture of an action that would make him or her feel that way. Discuss ways children can respond to the actions and feelings. Suggest that children draw responses on the same pieces of paper on which they drew the actions. Play this game when children have comfortable and uncomfortable feelings to encourage them to think before they respond and to respond in more positive ways.

Choices, Choices, Choices

Some children seem unaware that they have choices of how they can respond to actions and their feelings. They may make the same choices over and over again only because they don't know of other choices that are appropriate. Knowing they have choices gives children a feeling of control over their lives. Describe an action and feeling to children and then invite children to work in small groups to brainstorm appropriate responses. For example, ask children how they might respond if a younger brother or sister takes their toy and breaks it. A typical feeling may be one of anger. Some choices for responses may include crying, telling someone, breaking one of the sibling's toys, locking a door, helping the younger child learn how to play with the toy so it won't break, or telling the child how sad he or she is that the toy is broken. Invite each group to share their responses. Point out the variety of ideas. Encourage children to choose the most positive and constructive responses.

Making Wise Decisions

It's important to encourage children to decide how to respond to actions and feelings. The sooner they understand that they don't always have to make the same decisions when something happens repeatedly, the sooner they'll understand and take control of their own behaviors. As children make more and more decisions, they develop self-confidence about their decision-making abilities. Be sure to reinforce positive responses.

Give children opportunities to make some decisions. Begin with simple challenges, such as choosing between two books or three puzzles. Invite children to make choices throughout their day, such as deciding whether to play inside or outside or whether to wear sweaters or jackets. Gradually increase the decision-making challenges by giving children opportunities to choose between more options.

Attitude Alert

Explain to children that the word *attitude* means how they feel towards something or their current state of mind. Attitude involves a way of feeling—"I feel lazy when I watch TV." Attitude involves a way of thinking—"I think TV is a waste of time." Attitude also involves a way of responding—"I will turn the TV off." Attitude plays a major role in what children think of themselves and others.

The image of what children perceive they can and cannot do affects their entire being. Children who have poor attitudes tend to procrastinate, use self-defeating talk, and punish themselves with negative feelings. Often, they consider themselves failures. Children who have positive attitudes usually feel important, valuable, and worthy of respect by people who are important in their lives. They're usually optimistic and know they are capable of directing their lives and have the confidence to make decisions. Simply put, if children think they can, they usually can. If children think they can't, they usually can't.

Invite children to think about what type of attitudes or feelings towards things they usually have and how they feel about those attitudes by asking the following questions.
- How do you feel about things?
- How does your body show how you feel?
- What does your tone of voice tell about your attitude?
- How do you feel about your attitude or frame of mind?

What to Do: How Activities Help

Activities are an excellent way of encouraging children to express their feelings in positive and constructive ways. The practical activities in this resource guide help children understand their many different emotions. They reassure children that it is normal to have strong feelings. When possible, encourage active participation from all children. Children often learn best through hands-on activities. The activities in this resource are not intended to be a cure for children who have severe emotional or adjustment problems. These children may need to receive professional guidance.

Suggestions for Implementing the Activities

- Don't tell children how to feel or react. Like adults, children need to express their own feelings. Give basic directions, but allow children freedom to create their own projects with little outside interference. Their projects will be more meaningful to them if children create according to their own rules in a loosely structured environment.

- Provide a play environment in which activities can be introduced. This type of environment encourages children to approach feelings and thoughts that might otherwise be too uncomfortable to deal with.

- Some children choose to engage in one activity over and over and not to participate in others. That's okay. An activity may be perfect for one child and not useful for another. Feel free to rotate activities depending on the needs of the children.

- The thoughts and feelings children experience while participating in a project are important considerations. Encourage children to verbalize how they are feeling while participating.

The activities that follow explore the fourteen feelings presented in the children's book *Sometimes I Feel Awful*. After listening to children's comments and questions and helping them express how they feel, choose activities that are appropriate to meet each child's particular emotional needs.

Happy

**"Sometimes my days start happy . . . .
Today started happy. I had pancakes for breakfast,
I got to wear my favorite shirt, and
my friend David was coming over to play."**

These words from the book *Sometimes I Feel Awful* convey the initial happy feelings the young girl in the story has as she starts her day.

It's difficult for many children to understand that they can bring happiness to themselves. People and material items, such as toys, presents, or trips, bring only temporary happiness. Children can learn that they have an impact on their own long-term happiness. Explain to children that happiness can be having a positive attitude, viewing problems as challenges that can be conquered, or believing in oneself.

What Makes You Feel Happy?
Ask children what actions make them feel happy. Encourage children to discuss times when they felt happy and describe what happened to make them feel that way. Children might describe times when they baked cookies, played baseball, or talked with friends.

How Do You Respond?
Discuss responses children have to actions that make them feel happy. Children may respond by laughing, smiling, singing, skipping, or just playing with friends. Ask children how their bodies feel when they are happy. Children might notice that when they are happy, their bodies feel relaxed and energized. Compile the responses in a list on the chalkboard or on chart paper.

Making Me Happy
At times, children look to other people to bring them happiness. No one can make another person happy all of the time. Help children realize that they can bring happiness to themselves as well. Invite children to think of one thing they can do for themselves that would make them happy. Children may feel happier if they could learn to play new games, improve their athletic skills, or become better readers. Give each child a piece of paper and then challenge children to make lists or draw pictures of three or four things that would make them happy. Encourage children to keep their lists or drawings to refer to later.

Making Others Happy
People often feel happy when they are kind to others. Once children meet their need to feel good about themselves, they may increase their level of happiness by making others feel happy, too. Invite children to make friendship necklaces using colored cereal loops. Help children thread cereal loops onto pieces of yarn. Wind clear tape around one end of the yarn for easier threading. Be sure the yarn is long enough to slip over a child's head when the ends are

tied together. Encourage children to give the tasty necklaces to friends to wear and enjoy.

Happiness Is . . .

Encourage children to define what happiness is to them. Invite children to finish the sentence "Happiness is . . . ." Have children write or dictate their sentences on construction paper. Give children an opportunity to add illustrations to their definitions. Invite children to read their sentences aloud.

Jealous

**"When Mom left the room, I messed Tricia's
hair all up. Mom and Tricia didn't understand.
I could have said, 'Mom, I feel jealous.
Brush my hair, too.' But I didn't."**

These words from the book *Sometimes I Feel Awful* convey the jealous feelings the little girl has when her sister is receiving the attention that she wants.

Jealousy often accompanies low self-esteem. Children may feel they aren't as good as someone else or become jealous of possessions or attention another person is receiving. Often children are unaware of their jealousy or have trouble expressing it, so their response to the jealous feelings may include a negative or inappropriate response. A renewed feeling of self-esteem helps lessen jealous feelings.

What Makes You Feel Jealous?

Explain to the children that being jealous means wanting something that someone else has, such as a possession or attention. Ask children what makes them feel jealous. Encourage children to discuss times when they felt jealous and describe what happened to make them feel that way. Give examples yourself so children may become more comfortable sharing their feelings. Children might describe times when they were ignored or did not receive attention.

How Do You Respond?

Discuss the ways children respond to their feelings of jealousy. Start with your own responses to begin the discussion. Children may respond by complaining, crying, or saying mean things. Ask children how their bodies feel when they feel jealous. Children might notice that their bodies sometimes feel hot or tense or that they lack energy. Explain to children that it's okay to feel jealous. There is nothing wrong with feeling jealous. Help children understand that if they are uncomfortable with feeling jealous, they have the power to change their feelings. The next time a child feels jealous, encourage him or her to tell someone how they feel or find a friend to share with.

I'm Special

Jealous feelings often disappear when children's self-esteem is bolstered. Encourage children to make lists or draw pictures of what they feel is special about themselves. Add to children's lists by telling them what you think is unique or special about each one of them as well.

Others First

Encourage children to do something special for a person they feel jealousy towards. This sometimes helps the jealous child feel closer to or better understand the child he or she is jealous of. The child could offer to play a game with the other child, give that child a genuine compliment, or make the other child a special drawing or gift.

I Need You

If a child is suffering from jealous feelings because someone they care about is not spending enough time with them, help him or her find ways to tell that person how they are feeling. Suggest the child first practice telling his or her feelings to you. In other words, encourage the jealous child to express him or herself.

This Is What I Have!

Help children become aware of their special attributes or abilities. Invite children to bring something special that they have from home to show their friends. Or, encourage children to tell about non-material things they have—a best friend, a special story he or she wrote, an experience that was special, and so on. Challenge children to share their special things—teach a game, hang the special picture on the wall, help other children write their own stories, and so on. This activity helps children feel that they are special.

Impatient

"... I said, 'David, let's go climb the tree.'
David sat on the floor and put together my
dog puzzle instead. One more time I said,
'David, let's go climb the tree!"
David ignored me. So I punched him.
David didn't understand. I could have said,
'I feel impatient. I waited and waited for
you to climb the tree.' But I didn't."

These words from the book *Sometimes I Feel Awful* convey the impatient feelings of the little girl when she doesn't want to wait to do what she has planned.

Young children can be self-involved and impatient. They sometimes want immediate gratification of their basic needs—food, warmth, cleanliness, and love. Children learn more during the first six years of their lives than in any other period of their lifetimes. The more they learn, the better they are able to meet their own needs, and the less they have to rely on others. It may be hard for some children to understand that they may sometimes need to wait for things they want. As children become older and more independent, they generally become more patient with others as well as with themselves.

What Makes You Feel Impatient?

Explain to children that being impatient means feeling restless or unable to wait. Ask children what makes them feel impatient. Encourage children to discuss times when they felt impatient and describe what happened to make them feel that way. Share with the children a time when you were impatient. Children might describe times when they waited for their turn in line, when someone they were talking to was not listening carefully, or when they couldn't succeed at something new that they tried.

How Do You Respond?

Discuss responses children have to actions that make them feel impatient. Start with your own responses to begin the discussion. Children may respond by complaining, crying, or tapping their fingers or feet. Ask children how their bodies feel when they are impatient. Children might notice that they feel restless and that their hearts pound faster. Explain to children that it's okay to feel impatient. There is nothing wrong with feeling impatient. Help children understand that if they are uncomfortable with feeling impatient, they have the power to change their feelings. The next time a child feels impatient, encourage him or her to take a deep breath, count to ten, read, or tell the person they are waiting for how they are feeling.

Travel Bag

Most children learn to wait their turn and also learn to wait for others. But for some, waiting can be unbearable. For children who are impatient waiters, help them create a travel bag they can take along when they know there is a possibility they will have to wait for someone. Suggest the children put small toys, books, crayons, and coloring books in the bag for entertainment.

Count to Ten

Sometimes it can help when children have something to keep their minds busy while they are waiting. If possible, teach children to count to 5 or 10 in Spanish or French. Invite them to practice their new counting skills in a different language while in a situation that requires waiting.

English	Spanish	French
one	uno (OO-no)	un (uhn)
two	dos (dose)	deux (duh)
three	tres (trace)	trois (twah)
four	cuatro (QUA-trow)	quatre (KAH-truh)
five	cinco (SIN-ko)	cinq (sangk)
six	seis (sayce)	six (sees)
seven	siete (see-A-tay)	sept (seht)
eight	ocho (OH-cho)	huit (weet)
nine	nueve (new-WAVE-ay)	neuf (nuhf)
ten	diez (DEE-es)	dix (dees)

The Waiting Game

Play games with the children often, either board games or other games, where children have to wait their turn. Children can learn better waiting skills by playing these group games, as well as learning to share time with others.

Selfish

**"David picked up one of my games. I shouted,
'That's mine! You can't play with it.'
David didn't understand. I could have said,
'I feel selfish. That's my game. I don't want to
share it today. And besides, I still want to
climb the tree.' But I didn't."**

These words from the book *Sometimes I Feel Awful* convey the selfish feelings the little girl in the story feels when she doesn't want to share with her friend.

Some children are selfish because they have not been in an environment that requires sharing. A selfish child may have a family that does not share, so he or she may feel possessive. Selfishness is a natural emotion. Positive sharing experiences help children feel more comfortable when they share and can help children overcome their feelings of selfishness.

What Makes You Feel Selfish?

Explain to the children that being selfish means wanting things only for yourself or only your own way. Ask children what makes them feel selfish. Encourage children to discuss times when they felt selfish and describe what happened that made them feel that way. Describe your own feelings of selfishness as well. Children might describe times when someone took something that belonged to them without asking or when they were unwilling to share something they greatly valued.

How Do You Respond?

Discuss responses children have to actions that make them feel selfish. Start with your own responses to begin the discussion. Children may respond by crying, grabbing, tattling, or yelling. Ask children how their bodies feel when they are feeling selfish. Children might notice that their face gets red, their heart beats faster, or their muscles tighten. Explain to children that it is okay to feel selfish once in a while. There is nothing wrong with feeling selfish. Help children understand that if they are uncomfortable with feeling selfish, they have the power to change their feelings. The next time a child feels selfish, encourage him or her to explain to the other person why he or she doesn't want to share a particular toy or other object.

Share a Snack

Divide the group into pairs. Give each pair of children one snack (a cookie, handful of nuts, or raisins). Invite the children in each pair to divide the snacks and share with one another. Remind children to consider the other person as well as themselves, particularly if the snack cannot be divided evenly.

Giving to Others

Invite children to sort through their toys and clothes and consider which ones they may be able to give away to others. Donate the items to a non-profit organization or invite children to share the items with friends or other family members.

Thinking of Others

Encourage children to make an effort to think of others. Invite small groups of children to brainstorm lists of practical ways they can consider others. Children might suggest allowing someone else to get a drink first, go first in a game, or doing something nice for someone else, such as helping someone with homework, teaching someone a new game, and so on. Encourage children to put their ideas into practice.

Just for Me

Sometimes children need to feel that they have something special that no one else has. Invite children to make "Just for Me" boxes. Suggest that children bring toys, writing paper, or other special possessions from home to keep in their boxes. Let children know that the things in their "Just for Me" boxes are theirs and that they do not have to share these things with anyone else. Set aside independent time when children can use the items from their boxes. Remind children that they do not have to share, but they may do so if they like. It is their choice.

Angry

"Finally David was ready to go outside
and climb the tree. I was happy. On the way out,
he knocked over my block city. He tried to fix it.
I yelled, 'Get away from my blocks!' David
didn't understand. I could have said,
'I feel really mad. I worked hard to build that
city. Now it's ruined.' But I didn't."

These words from the book *Sometimes I Feel Awful* convey the angry feelings the little girl in the story feels when her friend accidently knocks over her block city.

Everyone feels angry at times and everyone expresses their anger in different ways. Many children express their anger in ways learned from their parents. Some children become loud and abusive—others may cry. Some children keep their angry feelings under control and then suddenly release their anger in destructive ways. Others keep their anger inside and withdraw, becoming silent and possibly self-destructive. Some children display anger because they feel unloved. Often, angry responses to situations provoke rejection from others, which only reinforces the feelings of feeling unlovable. Anger may also be repressed feelings of hurt. If children are taught to respond to hurt or unloved feelings in appropriate ways, it's possible to avoid angry explosions.

What Makes You Feel Angry?

Explain to children that being angry means being mad about something. Ask children what makes them feel angry. Encourage children to discuss times when they felt angry and describe what happened to make them feel that way. Share your own angry feelings that you have had as well. Children might describe times when a possession of theirs was taken without permission or a friend said something that hurt their feelings.

How Do You Respond?

Discuss responses children have to actions that make them angry. Start with your own responses to begin the discussion. Children may respond to anger by hitting, yelling, or slamming a door. Ask children how their bodies feel when they are angry. Children might notice that they feel sweaty, flushed, or shaky. Explain to children that it is okay to have angry feelings. There is nothing wrong with being angry. Help children understand that if they are uncomfortable with being angry, they have the power to change their feelings. The next time a child feels angry, encourage him or her to try talking with someone about how he or she feels, going for a walk, or hitting a pillow.

Write It, Toss It

Sometimes children have a hard time responding directly to the person with whom they are angry. Writing a letter can help release angry feelings. Suggest that each child write or dictate a letter that describes the actions of the person who made him or her angry. Encourage each child to include how he or she felt when the person did what they did and how the child would like the person to act in the future. After the letter is completed, have each child read his or her letter again to make sure he or she didn't forget anything. When the child is sure the letter is complete, he or she can deliver the letter to the person or just tear it up and throw it away.

Work It Out

Physical exercise can help children release tension that comes from feeling angry. Encourage children who are feeling angry to run laps around a track, do a series of jumping jacks, or participate in a timed relay. Be sure children understand that this is not a punishment for having angry feelings.

Punching Bags

Provide children who are feeling angry with some pillows or bags stuffed with newspaper. Encourage children to punch the objects and release their hostility. Remind children that even though it is okay to feel mad, it is never okay to hit another person when they are feeling angry.

Frightened

**"Finally David and I climbed the tree and
I was happy. We climbed higher and higher.
The branches started swaying and
I started crying. David didn't understand.
I could have said, 'I feel scared. It's too high.
Let's climb down.' But I didn't."**

These words from the book *Sometimes I Feel Awful* convey the frightened feelings of the little girl in the story when she climbs too high and is frightened by the experience.

Fear is a normal response to certain situations or behaviors. Fear is as much a part of life as pleasure and accomplishment. Children experience fear—ranging from feeling uneasy about what is going to happen next to the fear of being physically hurt. Some children fear change, such as changing schools, moving, or going somewhere they have never been before. Some children fear getting hurt, such as falling, dogs biting them, or getting a shot. Children sometimes fear being emotionally hurt—failing a test, being teased, or losing a friend. All of these fears affect children's self-esteem.

Fear, however, can also be positive. Apprehension prepares children to defend themselves or keeps them out of potentially dangerous situations. Encouraging children to talk about their fears and listening carefully to the children can help them learn how to respond to their feelings in positive and constructive ways. All of these fears are real to a child. We as adults need to respect and understand these fears, as well as help children find ways to alleviate them.

What Makes You Feel Frightened?

Explain to children that being frightened means feeling afraid or scared. Ask children what frightens them. Encourage children to discuss times when they felt frightened and describe what happened to make them feel that way. Express some of your own fears as well. Children might describe times when they were alone in the dark, visited a new place, or were threatened by bullies.

How Do You Respond?

Discuss responses children have to actions that frighten them. Start with your own responses to begin the discussion. Children may respond by denying they are frightened or by developing even more fears. Ask children how their bodies feel when they are frightened. Children might notice that their hearts pound faster or it may be difficult for them to move or talk. Explain to the children that it is okay to feel frightened or scared. There is nothing wrong with being frightened. Help children understand that if they are uncomfortable with being frightened, they have the power to change their feelings. The next time a child is frightened, encourage him or her to talk to someone about how he or she feels and find healthy ways to express or cope with his or her feelings of fear.

Monster Story

Some children are afraid of monsters. This is a very real fear for many children. The better children get to know the monsters they fear, the more they may understand what it is they are really afraid of. Invite each child to write or dictate a story about a make-believe monster he or she imagines. Encourage each child to include what the monster looks like, what its hobbies are, what it thinks about, and why the monster frightens people. Invite children to draw pictures to go with the stories. Encourage children to share their stories and pictures with others. Invite the class to ask questions, such as "Does the monster have a family?" "Is the monster happy? Sad? Angry?" and so on.

Trying Something New

Often, new experiences frighten children because they are afraid of the unknown. Give children opportunities to try new things, such as a game, sport, or even a food they have never tried before. Provide children with lots of encouragement. After children have tried the new experiences, talk about whether or not they are still afraid. Ask children why they aren't afraid anymore. Ask if they would like to try something else that's new. Encourage children as they continue to try new experiences.

Imagine the Best

Instead of asking children if they are frightened, ask how something makes them feel. "How do you feel when you walk into a dark room at night?" Often children think the worst. Chances are they think there is a monster or a burglar in the dark room rather than something positive. Encourage children to identify what is happening, what they are feeling, and then help them choose a positive way to respond to their feelings. "The room is dark and I feel safe because no one is in it," for example.

Sad

"... David said he didn't want to play
with me anymore. He was going home, he said,
because I was too cranky. ...
Wheaton tried to make me feel better,
but I shoved him away. I could have
petted Wheaton and said, 'I feel sad. David left.
You're my only friend.' But I didn't."

These words from the book *Sometimes I Feel Awful* convey the sad feelings the little girl has when things don't go the way she plans.

Some children show their sadness by crying. Others withdraw and don't show their sad feelings at all. It doesn't occur to many children that sharing their sadness can help the uncomfortable feelings go away. Burying unpleasant feelings never makes them go away. The harder children try not to feel sad, the more intense the feeling may become. Encourage children to share their feelings with others.

Sadness that lasts a long time may turn into depression. If this is the case, it may be wise to talk about the situation with the family or a professional.

What Makes You Feel Sad?
Ask children what makes them feel sad. Encourage children to discuss times when they were sad and describe what happened to make them feel that way. Share some sad feelings you have had as well. Children might describe times when a friend moved away, a loved one died, or even a time when they were not able to watch a favorite television show.

How Do You Respond?
Discuss responses children have to actions that make them sad. Start with your own responses to begin the discussion. Children may respond to sadness by burying their feelings, crying, or withdrawing. Ask children how their bodies feel when they are sad. Children might notice that their bodies feel tired, they can't concentrate, or they have no appetite. Explain to children that it is okay to feel sad. There is nothing wrong with feeling sad. Help children understand that if they are uncomfortable with feeling sad, they have the power to change their feelings, even if only for a little while. The next time a child is sad, encourage him or her to talk to someone about how he or she feels, do something kind for themselves, or do something he or she especially enjoys with a friend.

Sad Sock
For some children who are uncomfortable sharing sad feelings, a stuffed animal or puppet may help. Some children are more likely to open up to a stuffed animal because they know they will be listened to and not judged harshly. Help children make sock puppets. Invite children to stuff socks and add facial features using permanent markers. After children feel comfortable sharing their feelings with their hand-

made sock puppets, encourage them to open up to you or to any other person they might feel comfortable with. Children may first share with you or another person through the puppet, and then, if they feel comfortable, talk directly to you or another person.

Favor for a Friend

When children are sad, they often become introspective and see only their own situation or circumstances. Encourage children to take care of themselves, but also do something nice for someone else to get their minds off their sadness. Invite children to make a card or gift, write a poem, or do a special favor for a friend or family member. Explain to a sad child that it's okay to feel sad, but concentrating on something else may help them feel better for just a little while. Give children the option of going back to their feelings of sadness if they need to.

The Perfect Day

Invite children who are feeling sad to take a break from their sadness and set their minds on happier thoughts for just a little while. Encourage children to think about what a perfect day would be like for them. Have children write a paragraph or draw a picture that describes a perfect day.

Cranky

**"... I kicked the dirt, stomped into the house,
slammed the door, and shouted at Mom
as she talked on the phone. Mom didn't understand.
I could have said, 'I want to cuddle. I feel
cranky about David going home.' But I didn't."**

These words from the book *Sometimes I Feel Awful* convey the cranky feelings the little girl has because of her frustrations and disappointments.

It is not unusual for both children and adults to feel cranky, irritable, or out-of-sorts from time to time. A seemingly insignificant situation seems more annoying or offensive when children are cranky. Also when children are cranky, they are sometimes overly sensitive or cry easily. Sometimes it is best to distract or remove a child from the situation that is causing the annoyance when he or she is irritable.

What Makes You Feel Cranky?

Explain to children that feeling cranky means feeling cross, annoyed, or irritable. Ask children what makes them feel cranky. Encourage children to discuss times when they were cranky and describe what happened to make them feel that way. Talk about times when you have felt cranky as well. Children might describe times when a friend moved away, something didn't work out the way they wanted it to, or even a time when they didn't get enough sleep.

How Do You Respond?

Discuss responses children have to actions that make them cranky. Start with your own responses to begin the discussion. Children may respond by crying, hitting, saying mean things, or not listening to others. Ask children how their bodies feel when they are feeling cranky. Children might notice that their bodies feel tired, achy, or tense. Explain to children that it's okay to feel cranky. There is nothing wrong with being cranky. Help children understand that if they are uncomfortable being cranky, they have the power to change their feelings. The next time a child is cranky, encourage him or her to talk to someone about how he or she feels or take a deep breath and try to relax and rest.

Play with Clay

Encourage children to take their cranky feelings out on clay. Invite children to create people or objects or just simply squeeze, poke, and pound a clay ball.

Soothing Sounds

Play some soft, mellow music when children feel cranky. Invite children to sit in comfortable chairs or relax on the floor with pillows as they close their eyes and listen to the soothing sounds. Encourage children to visualize what the sounds make them think of as they relax.

Quiet Games

When children are cranky, have a time out and invite them to put together puzzles, look at pictures, draw, or read.

Lonely

" . . . I whined in my whiniest voice. Mom didn't
understand. I could have said, 'I feel lonely.
David went home and I don't have anyone
to play with.' But I didn't."

These words from the book *Sometimes I Feel Awful* convey the lonely feelings the little girl feels when she is left
alone to play all by herself.

Occasionally children confuse being alone with being
lonely. Some children are uncomfortable being alone
because they think there must be something wrong with
them if there aren't other people to play with. Sometimes
when children are lonely, they think they are unlovable or
unlikable. It's important for children not to let lonely
thoughts undermine their self-esteem. Encourage children to

talk about their lonely feelings with people they trust. Invite children to seek out things to do when they feel lonely, such as visit a friend, play with a pet, and so on.

What Makes You Feel Lonely?

Explain to children that feeling lonely means wanting company or a friend to talk to. Ask children what makes them feel lonely. Encourage children to discuss times when they were lonely and what happened to make them feel that way. Describe times when you were lonely as well. Children might describe times when a close friend moved away, others ignored them, or they had no one to play with.

How Do You Respond?

Discuss responses children have to actions that make them feel lonely. Start with your own responses to begin the discussion. Children may respond to loneliness by pouting, complaining, or talking negatively about themselves. Ask children how their bodies feel when they are lonely. Children might notice that sometimes they lack energy, feel scared, or feel tired. Explain to children that it's okay to feel lonely. There is nothing wrong with feeling lonely. Help children understand that if they are uncomfortable with being lonely, they have the power to change their feelings. The next time a child is lonely, encourage him or her to talk to someone about how he or she feels, find things to do that he or she enjoys doing by himself or herself, or make plans to do something with a friend.

Quiet Time

Encourage children to view their lonely times as opportunities to enjoy some quiet-time activities. Suggest that a lonely child read a good book, look through a photo album, or put a puzzle together. Invite children to make lists of other fun quiet-time activities to do when they are feeling lonely.

Be a Friend

Help children realize that to make friends when they are feeling lonely, they need to be friendly. Invite children to make a list of ways they can be friendly to others. Encourage children to put their friendly behaviors into practice.

Frustrated

"Mom handed me a picture to color. I scribbled all over it. Mom didn't understand. I could have said, 'Help me. I feel frustrated.' But I didn't."

These words from the book *Sometimes I Feel Awful* convey the frustration of the little girl when she can't color in the lines of the picture.

Everyone feels frustrated at times, although some children become frustrated more easily than others. Symptoms of frustration can include loud and aggressive behavior, lack of motivation, and negative attitudes. Positive reinforcement can help some children overcome frustration. By being successful, children's frustrations usually diminish.

What Makes You Feel Frustrated?

Explain to children that feeling frustrated means feeling helpless, feeling like they can't do something, or feeling discouraged. Ask children what makes them feel frustrated. Encourage children to discuss times when they felt frustrated and describe what happened to make them feel that way. Share some of your own frustrations as well. Children might describe times when they tried to put a puzzle together, fix a broken toy, or learn something new.

How Do You Respond?

Discuss responses children have to actions that make them feel frustrated. Start with your own responses to begin the discussion. Children may respond to frustration by crying, saying they can't do something, or pouting. Ask children how their bodies feel when they are feeling frustrated. Children might notice that their bodies may be tense when they are frustrated. Explain to the children that it's okay to feel frustrated. Help children understand that they have the power to make themselves feel better. The next time a child is frustrated, encourage the child to talk to someone about how he or she feels, take a deep breath, ask for help, or try the frustrating task a little later.

Watch It Happen

Suggest that children visualize themselves doing an action that usually frustrates them, such as riding a bike, reading, doing a math problem, and so on. Invite children to visualize themselves doing the task perfectly. Suggest that they draw a picture of themselves being successful. Encourage children to hang the pictures in their rooms or share them with friends and family members. Challenge the children to work towards being able to accomplish the task that is frustrating them.

Ask for Help

Encourage children to ask for help when they are feeling frustrated. Often, a little bit of assistance can eliminate prolonged frustration. Encourage children to learn to watch for others who appear frustrated and be willing to help them as well.

Leave It Alone

Sometimes a frustrated child needs to leave a task for a short time and come back to it later. Often a short break from an activity will give the child a more positive outlook toward trying again later. Suggest a quiet game for a child who is feeling frustrated.

I Think I Can!

If children think they cannot do something, they usually can't. But if they believe they can do something, they probably can. Read *The Little Engine That Could* (see the bibliography on page 61) to younger children. Help children understand how to think positively about themselves and their abilities when they feel frustrated.

Ashamed

"Mom took away the picture. She gave
Wheaton a dog biscuit and me a cookie and a
glass of milk. . . . I ate the cookie and spilled
my milk. I yelled at Wheaton and told
him he was bad. Mom and Wheaton didn't
understand. I could have said, 'I feel ashamed.
I'm sorry I made a mess.' But I didn't."

These words from the book *Sometimes I Feel Awful* convey the shame the little girl feels when she thinks she has done something wrong.

Children may feel a sense of guilt, disgrace, unworthiness, or inferiority if something they have done is perceived as wrong, improper, or silly. Some children may become too critical of their actions and feel ashamed more than is normal. The frequency of this emotion can affect a child's self-confidence and self-esteem.

What Makes You Feel Ashamed?

Explain to children that feeling ashamed means feeling that they have done something wrong or that they are not good enough. Ask children what makes them feel ashamed. Encourage children to discuss times when they were ashamed and describe what happened to make them feel that way. Describe times when you have felt ashamed as well. Children might describe times when they lied, lost a contest, or didn't finish something they promised to do.

How Do You Respond?

Discuss responses children have to actions that make them feel ashamed. Start with your own responses to begin the discussion. Children may respond by blaming others, denying they did anything wrong, or feeling sad. Ask children how their bodies feel when they are ashamed. Children might notice that they feel flushed, nervous, or embarrassed. Explain to children that it's okay to feel ashamed. There is nothing wrong with feeling ashamed. Help children understand that if they are uncomfortable with feeling ashamed, they have the power to change their feelings. The next time a child feels ashamed, encourage the child to talk to someone about how he or she feels, admit his or her mistake, apologize, find ways to correct the situation, or try to feel more positive about himself or herself.

I'm Sorry

Encourage children to admit or take responsibility for a situation when they have done something for which they feel ashamed. This may help children regain some measure of control over their feelings. Children may feel the need to apologize. Invite children to say "I'm sorry" only if an apology is appropriate. Never force a child to apologize. If it is forced, the apology will most likely be insincere because the child won't necessarily mean it.

Right the Wrong

If children have done something for which they are ashamed that has hurt the feelings of someone else, encourage them to right the wrong by expressing their feelings to the person harmed. Invite children to be honest with the person whose feelings they hurt.

Talking

Discuss feelings of shame more thoroughly with the children. Sometimes children feel ashamed about things that they don't need to be ashamed about. Explain to children that it is okay to talk to someone about feeling ashamed. Urge children to talk to someone they feel comfortable with about their feelings. Help children understand that you will not be critical or harsh if they want to share their feelings.

Shy

**"The day got even worse when my brother
came home from school. He brought home a
new friend. I hid behind the chair and
wouldn't talk. My brother and his friend didn't
understand. I could have said, 'I feel shy.
I don't want to talk to someone I
don't know.' But I didn't."**

These words from the book *Sometimes I Feel Awful* convey the shy feelings the little girl in the story feels when she is meeting someone new and doesn't feel comfortable.

Sometimes children are shy because they are uncomfortable, afraid, or have been taught not to speak when adults are present. Some children are simply quiet or have introverted personalities. There are many reasons for children's shyness. Some children may feel uncomfortable if they feel too much focus is on them. Shyness can also be a symptom of low self-esteem. If a child is overly shy, he or she may benefit from discussions or activities intended to bolster self-esteem.

What Makes You Feel Shy?

Explain to children that feeling shy means feeling uncomfortable or bashful around others. Ask children what makes them feel shy. Encourage children to discuss times when they were shy and describe what happened to make them feel that way. Talk about times when you have felt shy as well. Children might describe times when they entered a room full of people, had to speak in front of a group, or moved to a new neighborhood.

How Do You Respond?

Discuss responses children have to actions that make them feel shy. Start with your own responses to begin the discussion. Children may respond by hiding, not looking people in the eye, or not talking. Ask children how their bodies feel when they are shy. Children might notice that their bodies feel nervous or shaky. Explain to children that it's okay to be shy. There is nothing wrong with being shy. Help children understand that if they are uncomfortable with being shy, they have the power to change their feelings. The next time a child feels shy, encourage him or her to talk to someone about how he or she feels, try to answer when spoken to, and try to look directly at people who talk to them.

What's New with You?

To remove the focus off themselves, encourage shy children to interact more with others. Invite children to think of a list of questions they can ask to get to know someone better, such as "How many people are in your family?" "What's your favorite color?" and so on. Then divide the group into pairs. Ask one child from each pair to ask his or her partner the agreed-upon questions. Then have the children switch roles. This may help a shy child open up to one other person. This may also help shy children make new friends.

Play-Acting

Some children can set their shy feelings aside if they are pretending to be someone else. Encourage children to take part in skits or other forms of dramatic presentation where they are playing the part of another character. Some children may even feel more comfortable if they can wear a costume or mask.

Group Work

Give children the opportunity to speak in front of others, starting on a small scale. Begin by having shy children work with just one other person on a project. Then, for another project, have children work in groups of three, then four—gradually exposing shy children to even larger groups.

Left Out

**"... Mom and my brother talked to
each other in the kitchen. I jumped around,
made strange noises and weird faces.
Mom and my brother didn't understand.
I could have said, 'I feel left out.
Please talk to me, too.' But I didn't."**

These words from the book *Sometimes I Feel Awful* convey the feelings the little girl has when she is ignored.

Children often feel left out when they think they are not being accepted or not being heard by others. If children feel left out on a continual basis, it may affect their self-esteem. Help children find others with whom they can feel accepted who have common interests and abilities.

What Makes You Feel Left Out?

Ask children what makes them feel left out. Encourage children to discuss times when they felt left out and describe what happened to make them feel that way. Discuss times when you have felt left out as well. Children might describe times when they weren't included in a game, invited to a birthday party, or talked to.

How Do You Respond?

Discuss responses children have to actions that make them feel left out or ignored. Start with your own responses to begin the discussion. Children may respond by getting angry, becoming withdrawn, or feeling sad. Ask children how their bodies feel when they feel left out or ignored. Children might notice that their bodies feel flushed or shaky. Explain to children that it's okay to feel bad about being left out. There is nothing wrong with feeling bad about being left out. Help children understand that if they are uncomfortable with feeling left out, they have the power to change their feelings. The next time a child feels left out, encourage him or her to talk to someone about how he or she feels, try to join in, find new friends, or just play by himself or herself.

My Interests and Talents

Increasing children's self-esteem helps improve their comfort level with other groups of children. Have children make a list or draw pictures of their interests and talents. Invite children to share their lists or pictures. Draw attention to the similarities between children's interests.

Making New Friends

Encourage a child who is feeling left out or ignored to choose one person they do not know and make it a goal to introduce himself or herself to that person. Help the child plan what he or she will say and what he or she can do to make friends with another child.

Solo Games

Invite children to brainstorm a list of games they can play by themselves. Encourage children to use the time when they are not with friends to enjoy their time alone.

Tired

**"When it was time for dinner, I
didn't eat one bite. Today started happy and
turned into a jealous, impatient, selfish, mad,
scary, sad, cranky, lonely, frustrating, ashamed,
shy, left out, really tired day. Finally I said,
'I feel tired. I want to go to bed.'"**

These words from the book *Sometimes I Feel Awful* convey the tired feelings the little girl in the story has after her long and difficult emotional day.

When children are tired, a variety of emotions and responses can surface. Some children become sensitive or cry easily. Some children lack energy and seem listless. Others may appear lethargic or bored. The best way to handle tired children is to help them get the rest they need.

What Makes You Feel Tired?

Ask children what makes them feel tired. Encourage children to discuss times when they felt tired and what happened to make them feel that way. Talk about times you've felt tired as well. Children might describe times when they had to wait a long time, played hard all day, or were bored.

How Do You Respond?

Discuss responses children have to actions that make them feel tired. Start with your own responses to begin the discussion. Children may respond by crying, appearing listless, or being grumpy. Ask children how their bodies feel when they're tired. Children might notice that they feel weak or achy. Explain to children that it's okay to feel tired. There is nothing wrong with feeling tired. Help children understand if they are uncomfortable feeling tired, that they have the power to change their feelings. The next time a child feels tired, encourage him or her to talk to someone about how he or she feels, take a little rest, or eat a healthy snack.

Time Out

A five- or ten-minute rest can give children the added energy they need to make the rest of the day less difficult. When children seem tired, provide an opportunity for a quick rest. Invite children to get in a comfortable position on the floor and to be very still for five or ten minutes. Encourage children to let their minds relax and wander. Some children may not be getting enough sleep at home. You may need to contact the parents in these situations.

Healthy Snacks

Sometimes children feel tired and sluggish if they are hungry or have not been eating properly. Try to help the children eat a well-balanced diet. Provide them with healthy snacks, such as fruits, nuts, raisins, or juice. Make a special snacktime during the afternoon when you sense the children in your class are getting tired and need extra energy.

Additional Resources

Brown, Judith R. I Only Want What's Best for You. New York: St. Martin's Press, 1986.

This is a parent's guide to raising emotionally healthy children. The author helps adults avoid the traps that hurt children in the name of love.

Kellerman, Dr. Jonathan. Helping the Fearful Child. New York: W. W. Norton, 1981.

"How can I help my child feel comfortable about medical and dental visits?" "Is it normal for my seven-year-old to have nightmares?" "What should I do when my child has been frightened by something on TV?" Answers to questions and general principles supported by real-life examples are given to help parents deal with fears in their children.

Killinger, John. The Loneliness of Children. New York: Vanguard Press, 1980.

This book explores the isolation that children sometimes feel. Manifestations of loneliness are highlighted, as well as messages to parents and other adults about how to deal with their behaviors.

Klein, Carole. The Myth of the Happy Child. New York: Harper & Row, 1975.

Through the help of information gathered from interviews with children ages three to thirteen, the author reveals emotions natural to every growing child. The purpose of the book is to bring parents to a closer understanding of their children's emotions.

Zimbardo, Philip G. and Shirley L. Radl. The Shy Child. New York: Doubleday, 1982.

This resource provides guidelines in parenting styles, the role school plays in children's shyness, and other information in helping parents prevent and help their children overcome shyness.

Books for Children

Good children's books are excellent for stimulating conversation about feelings and emotions. Children, regardless of age, will usually respond by listening, thinking, imagining, and then expressing their thoughts. Reading a book about a similar experience that a child is facing can help him or her vicariously work through and solve his or her own problems. Reading helps children realize they are not alone.

The following is an annotated bibliography of some quality literature selections dealing with emotions that are appropriate for preschool to third-grade children. Choose the books that best suit the needs of the children in your care.

The Berenstain Bears Get the Gimmies
by Stan and Jan Berenstain
New York: Random House, 1988
The Berenstain bear cubs get that old gimmie gleam in their eyes every time they get in the checkout line at the supermarket. They whine and scream for everything they see and Mama and Papa bear usually give in to quiet them down. Papa finally explains to the cubs that their behavior is outrageous, disgraceful, and embarrassing. With the help of Gramps and Gran, the family works out a plan to cure the cubs of the galloping greedy gimmies.

I Was So Mad!
by Norma Simon
Niles, Illinois: Albert Whitman, 1974
In this story, young children describe various circumstances that make them mad—"I get mad when I try to tie my shoe." "I get mad when somebody says 'I bet you can't do this trick.'" and "I get mad when my brother goes to the ball game after supper and I have to go to bed." The story ends with the message that it is okay to be mad and everybody gets mad from time to time. Recognizing and verbalizing mad feelings can help. The book ends with a song children can learn called "There Was a Man and He Was Mad."

I Wish I Was Sick, Too!
by Franz Brandenberg
New York: Greenwillow Books, 1976

When Edward is sick, his family gives him the care and attention he needs. They serve him meals in bed and read him stories. Elizabeth becomes jealous of the attention he receives and wishes that she could be sick, too. A few days later, her wish comes true. She soon realizes that the grass is not always greener on the other side and that the best part of being sick is getting well.

It's Mine!
by Leo Lionni
New York: Alfred A. Knopf, 1985

On an island in the middle of Rainbow Pond lived three quarrelsome frogs. Milton insisted that the water belonged to him. Rupert declared that the earth was his. Lydia screamed, "The air is mine!" One day a huge storm darkens the sky and it begins to rain very hard. The island grows smaller and smaller as the water rises. The frightened frogs huddle together on one rock. They joyfully agree that the island belongs equally to them all. This story is a good lesson in sharing.

The Little Engine That Could
by Watty Piper
New York: Platt & Munk, 1961

Everyone wonders what will happen when the little train breaks down and cannot go over the mountain. But, with perseverance, the little engine makes it over. A good book about self-esteem.

The Luckiest of All
by Bill Peet
Boston: Houghton Mifflin, 1982

A young boy sitting in a tree makes guesses about who he thinks is the luckiest one of all. The boy thinks that being a bird is surely a better life because flying is such fun. However, the bird is quick to point out that feathered fun has its down side, too. The story delves into the inner desires of a variety of creatures.

Lyle and the Birthday Party
by Bernard Waber
Boston: Houghton Mifflin, 1966

Lyle is naturally a lovable and sweet-natured crocodile. But something happens when preparations begin for Joshua's birthday party. Lyle becomes jealous. By the time the party is over, the lovable green crocodile is in a dark and dreadful mood. The next morning, Lyle appears to be ill and is finally admitted to the hospital. While staying at the hospital, Lyle realizes that doing nice things for others makes him feel good again. He makes many new friends, his jealousy disappears, and an exciting surprise awaits him when he returns home.

Shy Charles
by Rosemary Wells
New York: Dial, 1988

Charles was as happy as he could be. However, Charles was terrified at the thought of meeting other children, talking on the phone, or even saying "thank you" to a family friend. One evening, Charles is faced with an actual emergency when his babysitter tumbles down the stairs. This shy, silent mouse springs into action and proves to be one of the biggest heroes of all. The real moral of the story is that it is okay to be shy.

There's a Nightmare in My Closet
by Mercer Mayer
New York: Dial, 1968

A boy is convinced there is a mean and frightening nightmare hiding in his closet. Each night before going to sleep, the child closes the closet door to keep the creature out of sight. One night, he decides to confront his fear. After meeting the creature face to face, the young boy realizes that the nightmare is timid and sensitive. The young boy ends up trying to comfort the creature. This story helps teach children that the unknown is not nearly as frightening once it is explored.

The Way I Feel Sometimes
by Beatrice Schenk de Regniers
New York: Houghton Mifflin, 1988

This book is a collection of poems that captures the changing emotions of children. The poems express children's feelings about glad days, sad days, and mixed-up-good-and-bad days. Children share their feelings about scary imaginary creatures, a new baby in the house, and waking up on the wrong side of the bed.

Why Couldn't I Be an Only Kid Like You, Wigger
by Barbara Shook Hazen
New York: Atheneum, 1977

Wigger never has to wear hand-me-down clothes or babysit a younger brother or sister. To a young child looking in, Wigger's life seems ideal. Being an only child seems to have all the advantages. At least, that is the way it looks from one side. However, Wigger looks at a different side of the issue as he explains that his life is sometimes lonely.

Will I Have a Friend?
by Miriam Cohen
New York: Macmillan, 1967

This is the story of Jim's first day at school. The biggest question on his mind is "Will I have a friend?" As Jim arrives at school and participates in classroom activities, he begins to feel as if all the friends are taken. He feels left out and alone. But, at the end of the day, Jim is happy to report to his Pa that he has a friend at school.

Will You Come Back for Me?
by Ann Tompert
Niles, Illinois: Albert Whitman, 1988

Suki's mother takes her to visit Mrs. Clara's Child Care Center. After spending an afternoon there together, Suki feels uneasy and tosses and turns in her bed that night. The next morning, Suki tells her mother about a dream she had. In the dream, Suki took her stuffed bear to a day care center and the bear cried when Suki started to leave her. Suki's mother realized that Suki feared she, too, would be left at the day care. So Suki's mother thinks of an idea to ease Suki's fears.

Index